stitch & sizzle
ACCESSORIES

stitch & sizzle
ACCESSORIES

hot handbags, scarves, wraps & accents

**Creative Publishing
international**

Chanhassen, Minnesota

Creative Publishing international
18705 Lake Drive East
Chanhassen, Minnesota 55317
1-800-328-3895
www.creativepub.com
All rights reserved

Creative Publishing
international

President/CEO: Ken Fund
Vice President/Publisher: Linda Ball
Vice President/Retail Sales: Kevin Haas

STITCH & SIZZLE ACCESSORIES

Executive Editor: Alison Brown Cerier
Managing Editor: Yen Le
Senior Editor: Linda Neubauer
Project & Photo Stylist: Joanne Wawra
Photographer: Tate Carlson
Production Manager: Helga Thielen

Cover Design: Q2A Solutions
Page Design & Layout: Yee Design
Samplemaker: Teresa Henn

Library of Congress Cataloging-in-Publication Data
Stitch & sizzle accessories : hot handbags, scarves, wraps & accents /
edited by Linda Neubauer.
    p. cm.
 ISBN 1-58923-207-0 (soft cover)
 1. Dress accessories. 2. Handbags. 3. Scarves. I. Title: Stitch and sizzle
accessories. II. Neubauer, Linda. III. Creative Publishing international.
 TT560.S74 2005
 646.4'8--dc22

                                    2005000211

Printed in China:
10 9 8 7 6 5 4 3 2 1

Contents

Stitch & Sizzle

Sewing and crafting fashion accessories is hot! So many people are making their own handbags and other accessories, and you can, too.

Stitch & Sizzle Accessories presents two dozen original designs that will definitely turn heads. With so many choices, where you will start? Will it be a shiny mini-bag? An elegant scarf? A whimsical tote? A sheer wrap for a big event? An embossed I.D. holder for work? These are fresh designs styled for casual fun, for career, or evenings and special occasions. Everything about these accessories sizzles: colors, fabrics, details! There are lots of trendy embellishments like beading and embossing, too.

Step-by-step instructions with photos and illustrations make the projects easy. If you have very basic sewing skills, you can make anything in the book. Since accessories are small projects, they're quick, too. Though easy to make, these are polished, designer-perfect accessories you will be proud to wear and use.

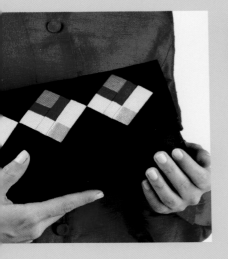  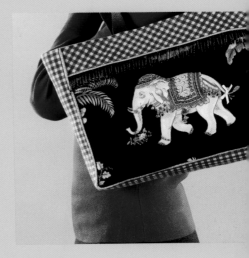

Bags & Totes

Ultra Bag

LINDA NEUBAUER

This is the ultimate everyday bag: ultra soft, ultra light, and ultra colorful. No wonder, as it's made of Ultrasuede, the amazing fabric that looks like fine suede but sews and washes like fabric. Ultrasuede is pricey, but you don't need very much—and besides, you're worth it! It comes in vibrant colors, like this orange. The bag is full of features inside and out, like the braided trim, and takes advantage of the handbag notions that are now widely available, like a magnetic snap and metal buckle. This is a real bag with a luxury look.

what SIZZLES

Ultrasuede, still hot after all these years

Handbags in bright colors

Luxury details that say, "Look at me!"

1. Enlarge and cut out the pattern pieces (page 15). Cut a front and back and two gusset pieces from the Ultrasuede. Transfer the dots to the wrong side of the bag pieces. Also cut two 2¹/₄" x 8³/₄" (6 x 22.4 cm) strips for the zipper, a 1¹/₂" (3.8 cm) strap of the desired length, a 2" x 6" (5 x 15 cm) strip for the tab, and a 1" x 8" (2.5 x 20.5 cm) strip for the tab braid.

2. Cut fusible fleece pieces for the front, back, and gussets. Trim ¹/₄" (6 mm) from the outer edges of all the fleece pieces. Fuse the fleece to the wrong side of the Ultrasuede pieces. Re-mark the dots.

3. Stitch the wide ends of the gusset together in a ³/₈" (1 cm) seam. Spread the seam allowances open and topstitch on each side of the seam.

4. Staystitch a scant ³/₈" (1 cm) from the edge between the dots on both sides of the gusset. Clip up to the stitching every ³/₈" (1 cm). Pin the gusset to the bag front, matching the dots and aligning the center bottom to the gusset seam. Stitch a ³/₈" (1 cm) seam. The gusset edge will spread at the clips to allow the gusset to fit smoothly at the curved corners. Start and stop stitching ³/₈" (1 cm) from the upper edges.

5. Turn the seam allowances toward the gusset. Topstitch along the seam on the gusset. Stitch the other side of the gusset to the bag back, and topstitch.

6. Fold the strap in half lengthwise and press. Topstitch along both edges. Center the ends on the upper edges of the gusset, right sides together, and baste in place.

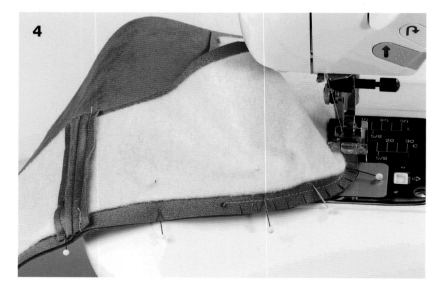

7. Fold the long sides of the tab to the center and press. Unfold the sides and install the male side of the magnetic snap into the center of the tab strip, 1 3/4" (4.5 cm) from one end, following the manufacturer's directions. Refold the tab sides and glue in place.

8. Cut the braid strip into three equal widths, up to 3/4" (2 cm) from one end. Place the uncut end of the braid strip over the end of the tab nearest the snap, covering the raw edges. Stitch the pieces together in a small rectangle. Braid the strip. Baste the free ends of the braid to the other end of the tab. Attach the buckle to the braid above the snap. Baste the tab to the center upper edge of the bag back, right sides together.

9. Press the zipper strips in half lengthwise. Place one strip over the right side of the zipper, with the fold near the zipper teeth. Topstitch in place. Repeat on the other side.

10. Turn the bag inside out and turn the strap and tab to the inside. Open the zipper partway. Stitch the zipper piece to the bag top, right sides together.

11. Turn the bag right side out. Close the zipper and pull the braided tab snug over the top. Mark for the placement of the female side of the snap on the bag front. Install the snap.

12. Cut a front and back from lining fabric. Cut one gusset piece by placing the center seamline on the fabric fold. Also cut two 6" x 12" (15 x 30.5 cm) pocket pieces.

13. Fold the pockets in half, right sides together, and stitch the sides. Turn right side out and press. Center a pocket on the lining front, aligning the lower edges. Stitch along the pocket sides. Baste the raw edges together at the bottom. Repeat for the back pocket.

Continued on next page>

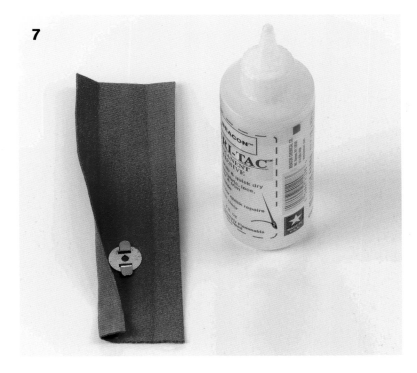

7

14. Stitch the gusset to the lining front and back as in steps 4 and 5 on page 12, leaving an opening along one side of the bottom for turning. Stop stitching $3/8$" (1 cm) from the upper edges.

15. With the bag and lining inside out, align the right side of the upper edge of the lining to the upper edge of the bag. Stitch the sides and ends. Pull the bag through the opening in the lining. Stitch the opening closed, and turn the lining down into the bag.

Bag Patterns

Copy at 200%.

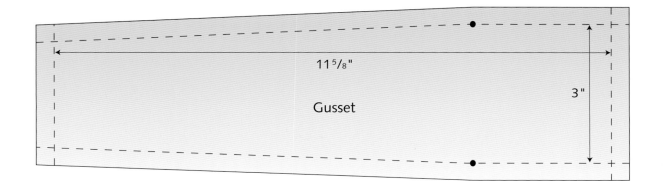

11⁵/₈"

Gusset

3"

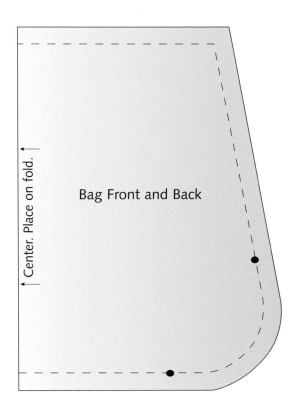

Center. Place on fold.

Bag Front and Back

Hot Buttons Bag

JOANNE WAWRA AND CAROL PILOT

Is someone or something pushing your buttons? Cheer yourself up with this playful bag. It's made of soft cotton velveteen shaped with a paper-bag bottom and dotted with colorful buttons. Clever handles are formed by stringing painted spools and beads on stiff wire. Pick wire that is firm enough to hold its shape, yet thin enough to go through the beads and spools. The bag is fully lined and has two inner pockets and a simple button closure.

what SIZZLES

Embellishing
with buttons

Clever handle of
beads and spools

1. Cut a 24" x 12" (61 x 30.5 cm) rectangle from the velveteen for the outer bag. Cut fusible fleece to the same size and fuse it to the wrong side of the outer bag.

2. Fold the outer bag in half, right sides together. Stitch the side and bottom together, using ¹/₂" (1.3 cm) seam allowances, and pivoting at the lower corner. Clip into the seam allowance at the corner fold. Press the seam allowances open.

3. Create a paper-bag bottom by aligning the side seam to the bottom seam and spreading the bottom

corner into a triangle. Stitch from fold to fold, perpendicular to the seam, 2" (5 cm) from the point. Repeat on the opposite side, aligning the side fold to the bottom seam. Trim off the triangles ¹/₄" (6 mm) from the stitching lines.

4. Cut one 24" x 12" (61 x 30.5 cm) rectangle for the lining and two 11" x 6" (28 x 15 cm) rectangles for the pockets. Fold the pocket pieces in half crosswise, right sides together. Stitch a ¹/₂" (1.3 cm) seam around the outer edges, leaving an opening for turning.

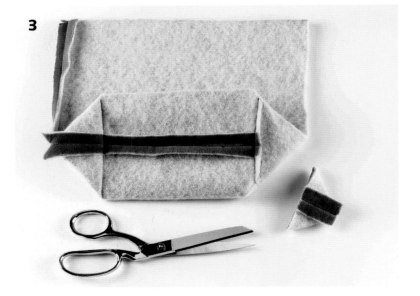

3

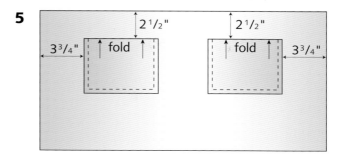

5 2½" 3¾" fold 2½" fold 3¾"

5. Trim the pocket corners. Turn the pockets right side out, and press. Pin the pockets to the lining fabric 2½" (6.5 cm) from the upper edge of the lining and 3¾" (9.5 cm) from the short sides. Edgestitch in place around three edges.

6. Follow steps 2 and 3 for the lining, leaving an opening in the bottom seam for turning.

7. Stitch buttons onto the right side of the purse as desired.

8. Slip the outer bag into the lining, right sides together, matching seams at the side; pin. Stitch a ½" (1.3 cm) seam, leaving ½" (1.3 cm) openings at the sides for inserting the handle. Press the seam allowances open.

9. Turn the bag right side out through the opening in the lining. Make a vertical 1" (2.5 cm) buttonhole in the center of the bag front, ½" (1.3 cm) below the upper edge.

10. Paint the spools and beads as desired. Cut 20" (51 cm) of wire. String the spools and beads onto the wire in the order shown on page 17. Bend the wire ends into loops.

11. Insert the wire loops into the openings on the sides of the bag. Secure the handle to the bag by stitching buttons on the inside and outside of the bag at each side, running the stitches through the loops.

12. Cut cardboard for the bottom of the bag 3½" x 8" (9 x 20.5 cm). Cover the cardboard with fabric, using fabric glue. Insert the cardboard into the bottom of the bag.

11

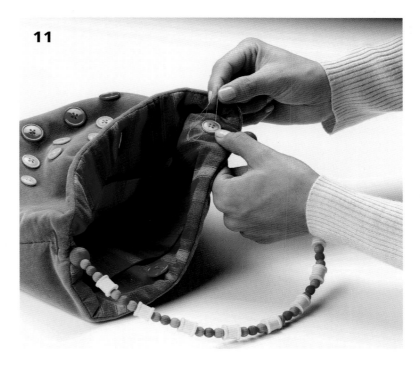

Drawn Together Bag

LINDA NEUBAUER AND TERESA HENN

This evening bag will draw lots of attention. Choose a fascinating silk brocade with an intricate motif like these dragonflies. The fabrics might be pricey, but you only need a little bit to make a big impression. If the brocade is reversible, you can use one side of the fabric for the outside of the bag and the other side for the lining. Otherwise, doupion silk in a coordinating color makes a gorgeous lining. You'll be amazed at how the bag is made; it's basically one square of fabric.

what SIZZLES

Intricate silk brocade

Clever design

1. Cut a 19" (48.5 cm) square from tracing paper to use as a pattern. Draw a stitching line ¹/₂" (1.3 cm) in from the edges. Mark dots on the stitching lines 6" (15 cm) from each corner. Connect the dots, drawing diagonal lines across each corner. These will become fold lines. Cut one square of outer fabric and one square of lining fabric. Mark the fold lines on the right side of the outer fabric. Remove the pattern.

2. Fold in the pattern corners on the marked lines. The stitching lines will form a cross shape. Trace the stitching lines onto another piece of tracing paper to make a pattern for the fusible batting. Cut one piece of fusible batting.

3. Cut a 3" x 6" (7.5 x 15 cm) rectangle from tracing paper. Round the edges slightly and trace the pattern onto the stencil plastic or cardboard. Cut out. This will be used to stabilize the bottom of the bag.

4. Center the plastic bottom on the wrong side of the outer fabric. Place the batting, fusible side down, over the outer fabric. The outer edges of the batting will be ¹/₂" (1.3 cm) from the fabric edges. Fuse the batting following the manufacturer's directions, being careful not to melt the plastic stencil material.

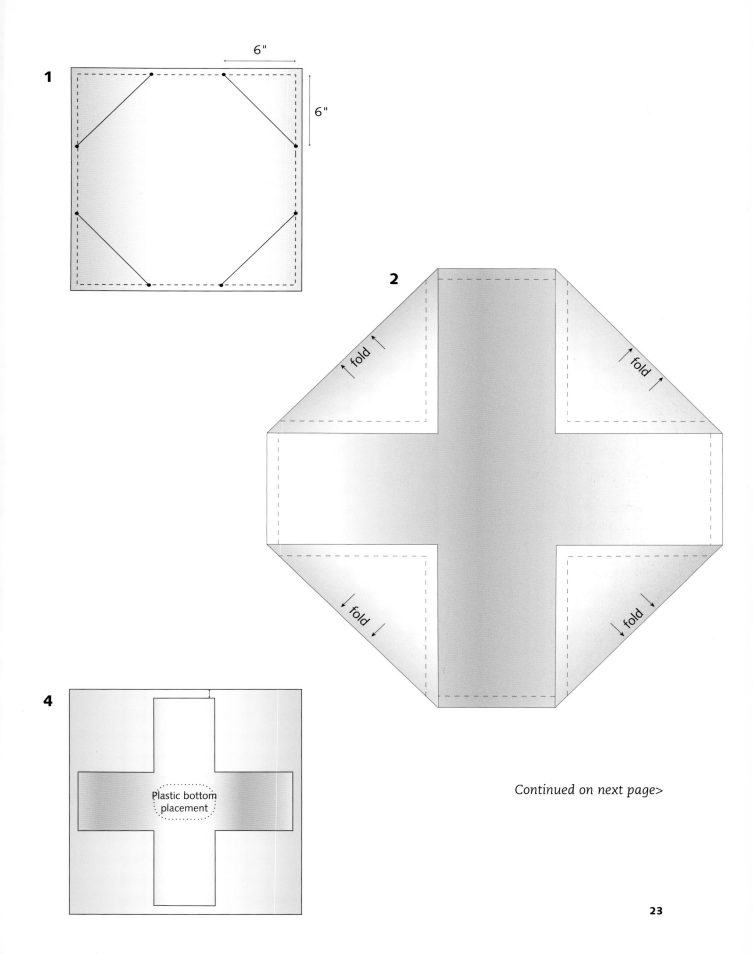

1

6"

6"

2

fold

fold

fold

fold

4

Plastic bottom placement

Continued on next page>

5. Place the outer fabric and lining right sides together. Stitch a $1/2$" (1.3 cm) seam around the square, leaving a 6" (15 cm) opening for turning. Clip the corners and trim the outer fabric only.

6. Peel the paper backing from the two 4" (10 cm) adhesive magnetic strips and center them in the seam allowance of the lining of the two straight edges that are parallel to the plastic bottom piece. This will become the bag closure.

7. Turn the bag right side out. Press, and slipstitch the opening closed.

8. Place the pattern for the plastic bottom over the plastic sandwiched inside the bag. Mark a line $1/8$" (3 mm) from the edge. Stitch through all the layers.

6

9. With the outer fabric facing up, fold back the corners and pin. Stitch a casing 1" (2.5 cm) from the fold on all four folded corners, backstitching at the beginning and end of the casing. Insert a grommet at each end of each casing.

10. Fold the bag in half, right sides together, aligning the sides with the magnetic strips. Tack the layers together on the sides, 1" (2.5 cm) from the center fold. Turn the bag right side out. Realign the magnetic strips.

11. Cut the cording in half. Thread one piece through the casings on one side of the bag, then from outside to inside through the grommets. Then insert the cord ends from inside to outside through the opposite grommets. Repeat on the other side of the bag.

12. Pull up the cords to gather the sides. Determine the desired length and knot the ends of the cords together.

To-the-Point Clutch

PATRICIA CONVERSE

The intricate design on the flap of this dressy clutch is a traditional quilt technique called Seminole patchwork. Bright Shantung fabrics—silk or synthetic—pop against a black background. On a practical level, lightweight, fusible interfacing makes the fabrics behave while you are cutting and stitching and provides structure for the clutch.

what
SIZZLES

Geometric design

Quilting

The nubby texture
of Shantung silk

Brights on black

1. Apply lightweight, fusible interfacing to the wrong sides of the fabrics that will be used for the Seminole piecing to stabilize them. Cut the following:

- one $1^1/_4$" x 7" (3.2 x 18 cm) strip of pink

- two $1^1/_4$" x 7" (3.2 x 18 cm) strips and one $1^3/_4$" x 7" (4.5 x 18 cm) strip of gold

- one 1" x 7" (2.5 x 18 cm) strip and one $1^3/_4$" x 7" (4.5 x 18 cm) strip of maroon

- one $1^1/_4$" x 7" (3.2 x 18 cm) strip of green

- two $2^3/_4$" x 7" (7 x 18 cm) strips, two $1^1/_2$" x 7" (3.8 x 18 cm) strips, and four 2" x 7" (5 x 18 cm) strips of black

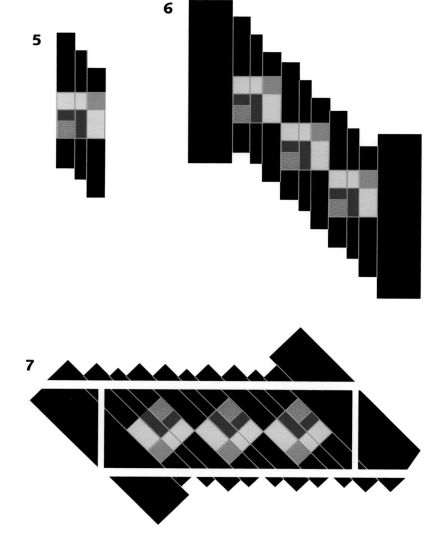

2. Using $^1/_4$" (6 mm) seam allowances, stitch a $2^3/_4$" black strip to a $1^1/_4$" gold strip to a 1" maroon strip to a $1^1/_4$" pink strip to a $1^1/_2$" black strip to make band A. Press all seam allowances toward the wide black strip. Cut three $1^1/_4$" (3.2 cm) segments from band A.

3. Stitch a 2" black strip to a $1^1/_4$" gold strip to a $1^3/_4$" maroon strip to a 2" black strip to make band B. Press all seam allowances toward the wide black strip. Cut three 1" (2.5 cm) segments from band B.

4. Stitch a $1^1/_2$" black strip to a $1^1/_4$" green strip to a $1^3/_4$" gold strip to a $2^3/_4$" black strip to make band C. Press all seam allowances toward the narrow black strip. Cut three $1^1/_4$" (3.2 cm) segments from band C.

5. Stitch a segment A to a segment B to a segment C, aligning the seams as shown, to make a block. Repeat twice to make three blocks.

6. Stitch the three blocks into a block strip, aligning the seams as shown. Stitch the remaining 2" (5 cm) black strips to the ends.

7. Trim $^1/_4$" (6 mm) beyond the block points at the top and bottom of the block strip, using a quilter's ruler and rotary cutter. Cut 1" (2.5 cm) from the end block points. The trimmed piece should measure $10^3/_4$" x $3^3/_8$" (27.3 x 8.5 cm).

8. Cut a 6" (15 cm) square and a 15" x 11" (38 x 28 cm) rectangle of light-weight, fusible interfacing, and fuse them to the wrong side of the outer fabric. Trace the gusset pattern from page 31, and use it to cut two gussets from the square fabric. Transfer the dot. From the larger piece, cut a $13^3/_8$" x $10^3/_4$" (34 x 27.3 cm) rectangle and a $1^1/_4$" x $10^3/_4$" (3.2 x 27.3 cm) rectangle.

9. Stitch the large rectangle to one side of the block strip, using a $^1/_4$" (6 mm) seam allowance. Stitch the narrow rectangle to the opposite side of the block strip. Press the seam allowances away from the block strip. Mark dots on the long edges $6^1/_8$" (15.4 cm) and $12^1/_4$" (31.2 cm) from the plain end; the first dot will align to the dot on the gusset, the second dot will align to the upper edge of the gusset.

10. Cut two gussets for the lining fabric; transfer the dots. Cut a 17" x $10^3/_4$" (43 x 27.3 cm) lining piece. Mark the long edges of the lining as in step 9.

11. Staystitch the outer bag a scant $^1/_4$" (6 mm) from the sides. Pin the gussets in place, matching the dots. Clip the seam allowances of the bag as needed to fit the gusset curve. Stitch the gussets to the bag, using $^1/_4$" (6 mm) seam allowances. Repeat for the lining.

Continued on next page>

12. Pin the lining to the bag, right sides together. Stitch ¹/₄" (6 mm) from the edges, leaving an opening in the plain short end for turning. Clip the seam allowances at the inside corner of the flap and gusset.

13. Turn the bag right side out and press. Edgestitch the plain short end, closing the opening.

14. Fold each gusset top right sides together, forming a pleat; pin. Stitch in place.

Gusset Pattern

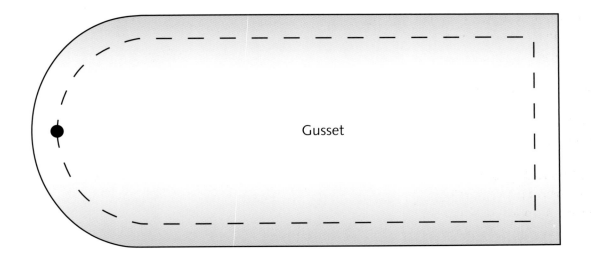

Gusset

Crackle Mini Tote

ELAINE JACKSON

Everybody needs a fun, bright tote. This crafty one looks like oilcloth or leather, but it's actually made of blackout drapery lining! The wrong side of the drapery lining, which has a smooth coating, becomes the outside of the tote. A textured surface is created with paint, stamping, and crackling. The tote is put together with hand stitches and a little glue—no sewing machine needed.

what
SIZZLES

A crackling hot
surface texture

Fun totes

you will need

- ¹/₂ yd. (0.5 m) blackout drapery lining

- Scissors

- Delta Ceramcoat acrylic paints in magnolia white, apple green, Seminole green, dark foliage green, rouge, Moroccan red, and fire red

- Artist's paintbrushes

- Chunky foam tulip stamp

- Palette or paper plate

- Blending gel medium

- Delta 2-Step Fine Crackle Finish

- Soft synthetic paintbrush

- Clean cotton rag

- Matte varnish

- DMC #5 perle cotton, color #988

- Sharp-point needle with large eye

- Fabric glue

- Clothespins

1. Cut out the following pieces for the tote from drapery lining:

- two 11" x 10" (28 x 25.5 cm) pieces for the front and back

- two 11" x 4" (28 x 10 cm) pieces for the sides

- one 10" x 4" (25.5 x 10 cm) piece for the bottom

- two 5³/₈" x 8" (13.7 x 20.5 cm) pieces for pockets

- one 22" x 3" (56 x 7.5 cm) piece for the straps

2. Paint one side of each piece with apple green paint. Dilute the paint slightly by dipping the brush in water. Allow to dry. Then paint the other sides.

3. Using a paintbrush, apply rouge paint to the blossom part of the tulip stamp and dark foliage green to the leaves. Stamp the right (smooth) side of the tote front in the upper center, with the tulip at a slight diagonal. This is the focal point.

4. Continue stamping tulips over the front of the bag, spacing them as shown on page 33. Stamp all the remaining pieces. Allow to dry.

5. Pour puddles of Moroccan red paint and blending medium onto a palette or paper plate. Dip the left side of a flat artist's paintbrush into the red paint; dip the other side into the blending medium. Brush a few strokes in the same direction on the palette to blend the color. Shade the left side of each tulip blossom. Shade the left side of the stems and leaves in the same way, using the dark green paint.

6. Highlight the right sides of the tulips and leaves with white paint. Allow all to dry.

7. Using a soft synthetic paintbrush, apply step 1 of the crackle finish evenly over the right sides of all the pieces. The thicker the coat, the larger the crackle. Allow to dry, following manufacturer's directions.

8. Using a soft synthetic paintbrush, apply step 2 of the crackle finish evenly over each piece. Fine cracks will begin to appear. Allow to dry flat overnight.

9. Using a clean cotton rag, rub dark paint into the cracks (dark red over the blossoms, dark green over the leaves, and seminole green over the background). Allow to dry.

10. Apply two or three coats of matte varnish over all the pieces, allowing to dry between coats.

11. Thread a needle with perle cotton and knot the end. Anchor the knot at the back of a pocket. Blanket-stitch around the pocket. Repeat for the second pocket. Glue the pockets to the wrong sides of the tote front and back, applying thin lines of fabric glue to the pocket sides and bottom.

12. Blanketstitch the tote side pieces to the sides of the front and back. Then stitch the tote bottom in place. Blanketstitch around the upper edge.

13. Cut the strap piece in half lengthwise. Fold each strap in half lengthwise and blanketstitch the raw edges together. Glue the strap ends to the wrong sides of the tote front and back, using a generous amount of fabric glue. Hold in place with clothespins until dry.

11

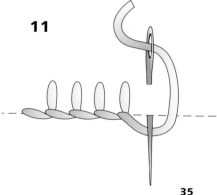

Glam Shopping Bag

JOANNE WAWRA AND TERESA HENN

Turn a few heads at the mall with a one-of-a kind tote made from a novelty print decorator fabric. Browse the home décor fabric section for large, isolated motifs with interesting details that can be enhanced with beads, sequins, and tiny bows. Animal images, like this glamorized elephant, always get attention. Coordinating fabrics are used for the top band, gusset, and piping as well as the lining, which features a zippered pocket.

what SIZZLES

Décor fabrics with whimsical motifs

Playful highlights of beads and embellishments

- $\frac{1}{2}$ yd. (0.5 m) novelty print decorator fabric

- 1 yd. (0.92 m) fusible hair canvas

- Assorted embellishments, such as beads, sequins, bell caps, and $\frac{1}{16}$" (1.5 mm) ribbon, as desired

- Beading needle and thread

- $\frac{1}{4}$ yd. (0.25 m) coordinating fabric for gusset and top band

- 1 yd. (0.92 m) fabric for lining and piping

- 3 yd. (2.75 m) cording, $\frac{3}{32}$" (2.3 mm) diameter, for piping

- Fabric glue stick

- 1 yd. (0.92 m) beaded fringe

- $1\frac{1}{4}$ yd. (1.15 m) nylon strapping, 1" (2.5 cm) wide

- 7" (18 cm) zipper

1. Cut two 13$\frac{1}{2}$" x 11" (34.3 x 28 cm) rectangles of the novelty print fabric for the front and back, centering the desired motifs. Note that the top 2$\frac{1}{2}$" (6.5 cm) of the front and back will be covered by the contrasting bands. Cut matching pieces of fusible hair canvas, and fuse them to the wrong sides of the fabric.

2. Highlight details of the novelty print with sequins, beads (page 91), and bows. Sew the sequins using a seed bead and a stop stitch. Outline and fill in areas using a backstitch. Make bead and bell cap dangles. Tie tiny bows and secure them to the fabric by tacking through the knotted center.

3. Cut two 3" x 13$\frac{1}{2}$" (7.5 x 34.3 cm) bias pieces of coordinating fabric for the top bands and one 4$\frac{1}{2}$" x 33$\frac{1}{2}$" (11.5 x 85.3 cm) straight-grain strip for the gusset. Cut matching pieces of fusible hair canvas, and fuse them to the wrong sides of the pieces.

4. Cut 3 yd. (2.75 m) of bias strips, 1$\frac{1}{4}$" (3.2 cm) wide for piping. Cut the strip ends on the straight grain and join strips end to end. Cover the cording to make the piping.

5. Attach the piping $\frac{1}{2}$" (1.3 cm) from one long edge of each bias band. Pull out and cut off $\frac{1}{2}$" (1.3 cm) of cording at each end to reduce bulk in the seam allowance. Glue-baste the heading of the bead fringe to the seam allowance, aligning the lower edge of the heading to the stitching line.

6. Fold under the seam allowance, so the beads extend downward. Pin the bands to the upper edges of the front and back, aligning the raw edges. Stitch in the ditch between the piping and the band.

7. Attach piping to the long edges of the gusset. Pull out and cut off $\frac{1}{2}$" (1.3 cm) of cording at each end to reduce bulk in the seam allowance. Stitch the gusset to the sides and bottom of the front panel with $\frac{1}{2}$" (1.3 cm) seam allowances. Clip the gusset seam allowance to the pivot points at the corners. Stitch the other side of the gusset to the back panel.

8. Cut the nylon strapping in half to make two handles. Baste the handle ends to the upper edge of the front and back 4" (10 cm) from the sides.

9. Cut two 13" x 11" (33 x 28 cm) rectangles for the lining front and back. Cut a 4^1/$_2$" x 33^1/$_2$" (11.5 x 85.3 cm) lining gusset and an 8^1/$_2$" x 12" (21.8 x 30.5 cm) pocket.

10. Mark a ^{1}/$_2$" x 7" (1.3 x 18 cm) zipper window on the wrong side of the pocket, 1" (2.5 cm) from one narrow end. Center the pocket on the front lining piece, right sides together with the raw edge 2^1/$_2$" (6.5 cm) below the top. Stitch on the marked lines, pivoting at the corners. Slash down the center of the rectangle and diagonally into the corners.

11. Turn the pocket to the inside, and press around the zipper window. Center the zipper under the window and glue-baste in place. Edgestitch around the zipper.

12. Fold the lower edge of the pocket up to meet the upper edge, right sides together. Stitch around the outer edges of the pocket only.

13. Stitch the lining gusset to the lining front and back, leaving an opening in one bottom seam for turning the bag right side out.

5

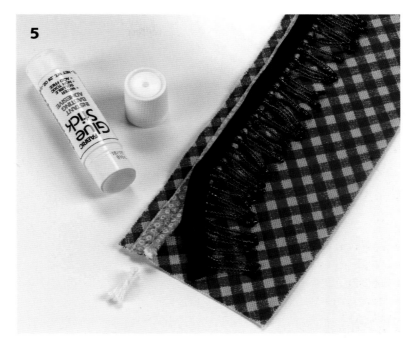

10

14. Stitch the lining to the tote along the upper edge, right sides together, using a ^{1}/$_2$" (1.3 cm) seam allowance. Turn the tote right side out through the opening. Stitch the opening closed.

15. Topstitch ^{1}/$_4$" (6 mm) from the upper edge of the tote.

39

Needle Arts Tote-along

JOANNE WAWRA AND TERESA HENN

Knitting, crochet, and embroidery are hot! People take their projects everywhere, and if you do too, make yourself the ideal tote. There is a wide inner pocket for stowing your instructions, a long side pocket for knitting needles and crochet hooks, and a zippered pocket for small notions, like a stitch counter, cable needles, a tape measure, or small scissors. The design of the tote is inspired by the needle arts, too. It features felted wools and a clever design of coils. Wood handles are anchored to the tote with wool felt ties.

you will need

- ⁵/₈ yd. (0.6 m) felted wool, 54" (137 cm) wide

- ¹/₈ yd. (0.15 m) felted wool in each of three accent colors, 54" (137 cm) wide

- Nylon netting

- Black permanent marker

- Water-soluble marking pen

- Variegated embroidery thread

- Open-toe embroidery foot

- ⁵/₈ yd. (0.6 m) fusible fleece

- 1 yd. (0.92 m) lining fabric

- 7" (18 cm) zipper

- One pair of purchased handles, 13" (33 cm) wide

- Cardboard

- Fabric glue

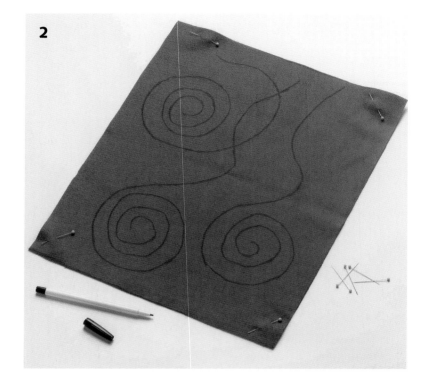

1. Steam the felted wools well to preshrink them. Cut two 13¹/₂" x 16¹/₂" (34.3 x 41.8 cm) pieces for the front and back. Cut a 4" x 45¹/₂" (10 x 116 cm) strip for the gusset. Cut a ¹/₄" x 54" (6 mm x 137 cm) strip of each accent color for the couched design and two ¹/₂" x 12" (1.3 x 30.5 cm) strips of each for the handle ties.

2. Enlarge the design pattern (page 45). Tape nylon netting over the pattern and trace it with a permanent marker. Pin the netting pattern to the right side of the tote front and transfer the design by drawing through the netting with a water-soluble marking pen.

3. Thread the sewing machine with variegated thread. Set the machine to stitch a multistitch zigzag (serpentine) with a 4 mm width and 2 mm length. Attach an open-toe embroidery foot. Couch the wool strips onto the tote front, guiding the strip between the toes of the presser foot. In areas of sharp curves, it may be necessary to stop several times with the needle down in the fabric, raise the presser foot, and turn the fabric.

4. Cut fusible fleece 1" (2.5 cm) smaller in both directions for the front and back and for the gusset. Fuse the fleece to the wrong sides of the tote pieces, leaving $1/2$" (1.3 cm) margins. Use a damp press cloth and lots of steam to ensure an even bond.

5. Pin the gusset to the tote front, wrong sides together. With the gusset facing up, stitch $1/4$" (6 mm) seams, using a straight stitch. Clip the gusset at the lower corners to allow the gusset to turn the corner smoothly. Stitch the opposite side of the gusset to the tote back.

6. Cut two $13 1/2$" x $16 1/2$" (34.3 x 41.8 cm) lining pieces for the front and back. Cut a 4" x $45 1/2$" (10 x 116 cm) strip for the lining gusset. Cut one $10 1/2$" x 13" (26.7 x 33 cm) piece for the book pocket, one $8 1/2$" x 12" (21.8 x 30.5 cm) piece for the zippered pocket, and one 4" x 31" (10 x 78.5 cm) piece for the side needle pocket.

7. Turn under and stitch a $1/2$" (1.3 cm) double-fold hem at the top of the book pocket. Turn under the sides and bottom $1/4$" (6 mm). Pin the pocket to the right side center of the lining front, 3" (7.5 cm) below the upper edge. Stitch in place.

8. Fold the needle pocket in half crosswise, right sides together. Stitch a $1/4$" (6 mm) seam in the short edges; leave the long side edges open. Turn right side out and press. Pin the pocket to the right side of one end of the gusset, 1" (2.5 cm) from the end, aligning the raw edges. Stitch the pocket to the gusset across the pocket bottom. Baste along the raw edges.

9. Sew the zipper pocket into the lining back, following steps 10 to 12 for the Glam Shopping Bag (page 39).

10. Stitch the lining pieces right sides together.

11. Slip the lining inside the tote. Turn under the upper edge of the lining, $1/4$" (6 mm) below the upper edge of the felt. Pin in place. Slipstitch.

Continued on next page>

12. Serpentine-stitch down the center of each handle tie, using the same setting as for couching. Mark positions for the ties on the tote front and back, 1" (2.5 cm) from the upper edges, using the handles as guides. Stitch across the center of each tie to secure. Tie the handles onto the bag.

13. Cut cardboard for the bottom of the tote 3 1/2 " x 13" (9 x 33 cm). Cover the cardboard with lining fabric, using fabric glue. Insert the cardboard into the bottom of the bag.

Design Pattern

Copy at 200%.

Bare Essentials Bag

JOANNE WAWRA AND CAROL PILOT

When all you need is a cell phone, lipstick, and a little cash, this splashy little flip-over bag has you covered. Made of sparkly metallic knit fabric with a thin shoulder cord, the bag is flexible and light. You'll hardly know the bag is dangling at your side as you mix and mingle. Inside the flap is a zippered pocket for a driver's license and cab fare.

what SIZZLES

Sparkling metallics

Beaded fringe

Taking along just the bare essentials

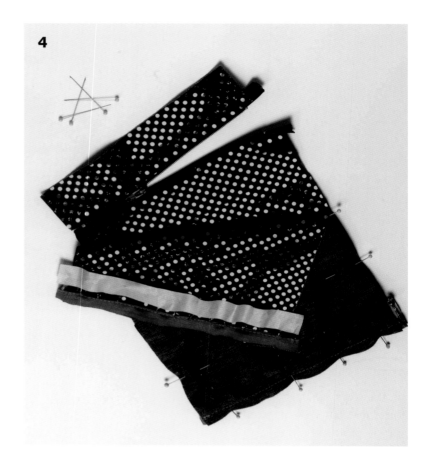

4

you will need

- ³/₈ yd. (0.35 m) medium-weight metallic knit fabric

- ³/₈ yd. (0.35 m) fusible knit interfacing

- Chalk or marking pen

- 7" (18 cm) zipper

- Zipper foot

- ¹/₂ yd. (0.5 m) beaded trim

- Masking tape

- 1¹/₄ yd. (1.15 m) cording

- Bodkin or safety pin

1. Cut one 11" x 8" (28 x 20.5 cm) rectangle of fabric for the outer bag; cut an 11¹/₂" x 8" (29.3 x 20.5 cm) rectangle for the lining. Cut a 10" x 8" (25.5 x 20.5 cm) rectangle for the pocket. Cut rectangles of fusible knit interfacing to match the outer bag and lining; fuse in place.

2. Mark a line 2" (5 cm) from one end of the lining; cut on the line. Align the narrow strip to the zipper tape edge, right sides together, and stitch within ¹/₈" (3 mm) of the teeth. Stitch the other side of the zipper to the cut edge of the larger lining piece.

3. Cut two lengths of beaded trim to fit the short ends of the outer bag. Pin in place with beads extending inward and the edge of the tape aligned to the raw edge of the fabric. To keep the beads from getting in the way when stitching, tape them down with masking tape. Baste as close as possible to the beaded edge of the tape, using a zipper foot.

4. Place the lining faceup on the work surface; open the zipper partway. Fold the pocket piece in half, wrong sides together. Place the pocket over the lining on the end opposite the zipper, aligning raw edges. Place the outer bag facedown over the pocket and lining. Pin the layers together.

5. Mark the outer edges 4" and 4½" (10 and 11.5 cm) from the top. The space between the marks will remain open for the cord casing.

6. Stitch the layers together ½" (1.3 cm) from the outer edge, leaving openings on the sides for the casing. Use a zipper foot, and stitch carefully over the basting lines next to the bead trim.

7. Trim the corners diagonally. Turn the bag right side out through the zipper. Remove the masking tape. Press lightly.

8. To make the casing for the handle, draw parallel lines across the inside of the bag connecting the ½" (1.3 cm) openings. Stitch on the lines though all layers.

9. Thread the cording through the casing, using a bodkin or safety pin. Overlap the ends and whip-stitch them together. Pull the joined area back into the casing so the ends are hidden. Stitch across the open ends of the casing to secure the cording.

9

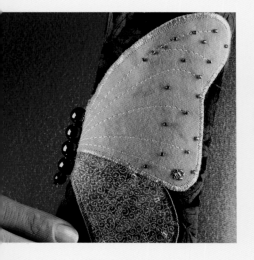  

Mini Bags & Accessories

Bedazzling Bag for Glasses

PATRICIA CONVERSE

This little pouch looks more like jewelry than a bag for eyeglasses. The butterfly design is a creative appliqué with tiny beads. The bag is quilted and softly padded, creating an accessory that is both useful and decorative.

what
SIZZLES

Sophisticated
butterfly design

Decorative stitching
and beaded accents

- Two coordinating fabrics for background and lining, 10" x 10" (25.5 x 25.5 cm) of each

- Two coordinating fabrics for wings, 5" x 10 " (12.7 x 25.5 cm) of each

- Quilter's safety pins

- Paper-backed fusible web, 10" x 10" (25.5 x 25.5 cm)

- Tear-away stabilizer, 10" x 10" (25.5 x 25.5 cm)

- Cotton embroidery thread; silver and iridescent threads, for decorative stitching

- Appliqué presser foot

- Light cotton batting, 10" x 15" (25.5 x 38 cm)

- Cotton thread to coordinate with background for construction and quilting

- Hand needle for beading

- Lightweight beading wire

- Beads: 16" (40.5 cm) strand each of 8-mm hematite and 6-mm cobalt; one small package each of Delica seed beads in silver hex cut and dark cobalt

1. Wash, dry, and press all the fabrics. Shrink the batting according to the manufacturer's directions, if desired.

2. Trace the bag patterns (page 56); cut out. Place the pattern pieces on the right side of the background fabric, right side up, and trace around them.

3. Trace the wing patterns (page 57); cut out. Trace the patterns for one upper and one lower wing onto the paper backing of the fusible web. Turn the patterns over and trace a mirror image set of wings. Fuse the web to the wrong side of the wing fabrics. Cut out the wings; remove the paper backing.

4. Fuse the wings to the bag, using the pattern as a guide. The upper wings should overlap the lower wings slightly. Note that the edges of the wings must be at least 1/4" (6 mm) from the edges of the bag to allow for the seam.

5. Place a 10" (25.5 cm) square of tear-away stabilizer behind the bag fabric. Thread the machine with cotton embroidery thread, and set the machine for a scant 1/8" (3 mm) wide satin stitch. Satin-stitch around the outer edge of the lower wings, beginning and ending at the points where they meet the upper wings. Pull thread tails to the back; knot and cut.

6. Satin-stitch the upper wings, using iridescent thread. Use a slightly wider stitch along the upper edge. Straight-stitch veins on the wings as desired. Carefully tear away the stabilizer.

7. Smooth the background fabric over a 10" (25.5 cm) square of batting. Baste it in place using safety pins. Thread the machine with cotton thread. Stitch tightly around the wings to create a shadow effect. Then stitch two to three rows of echo quilting around each wing pair.

8. Cut out the bag front and back on the marked lines. Place the pattern pieces on the wrong side of the lining fabric and cut them out.

9. Pin the lining front to the bag front along the top edge, right sides together. Stitch a 1/4" (6 mm) seam. Repeat with the back pieces. Clip up to the stitches at the point of the front seam.

10. Open the pieces. Pin the front to the back, right sides together, aligning the edges and matching the seams. Stitch a 1/4" (6 mm) seam, leaving an opening in the lining for turning. Turn right side out.

11. Thread a hand needle with a double black thread; knot the end. Insert the needle through the opening in the lining, and bring it through the bag seam to the right side at the position for the head bead. Put one 8-mm hematite bead on the thread, and backstitch. Repeat with three more hematite beads. Put one 6-mm cobalt bead and a silver seed bead on the thread. Insert the thread back through the cobalt bead and the last hematite bead. Bring the thread back to the inside, and knot.

12. Sew cobalt seed beads on the upper wings. Sew silver hex cut beads on the lower wings.

13. Cut beading wire about 30" (76 cm) long; thread it on a hand needle and make a large knot in the end. Bring the wire to the outside at the upper edge side seam. String a pleasing pattern of assorted beads until the necklace is the desired length. Bring the needle to the inside at the opposite upper edge side seam and knot securely on the inside.

14. Slipstitch the lining opening closed. Push the lining inside the bag.

11

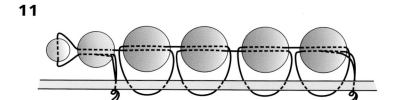

Bag Patterns

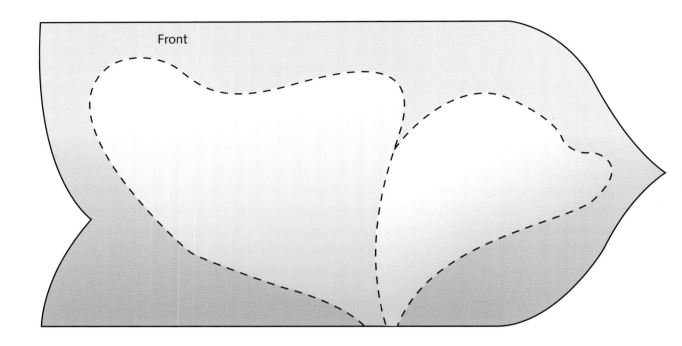

Front

Opening in lining for turning

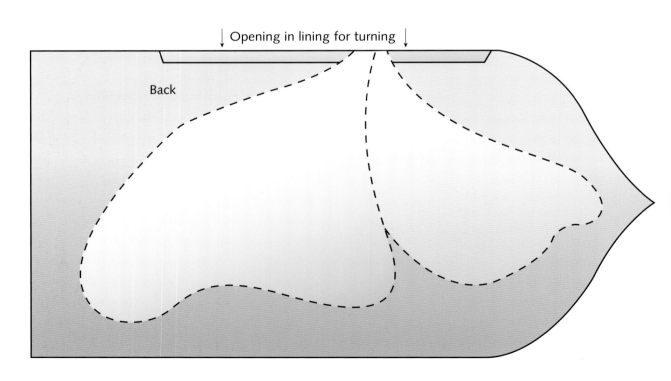

Back

Wing Patterns

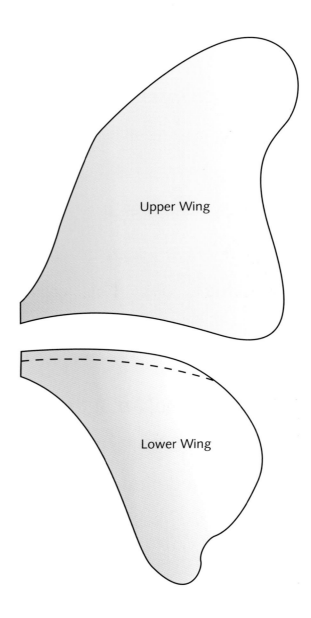

Upper Wing

Lower Wing

Badge Holder with Panache

PATRICIA CONVERSE

Do you have to wear an I.D. at work, or do you often attend conventions or trade shows where you wear a badge? Let's face it, an I.D. on a chain can really kill your fashion look. This classy badge holder is a brilliant solution. Made of metallic-stamped suede, it has a clear vinyl pocket to hold that badge, plus two zippered pockets to carry business cards, money, or a note pad.

you will need

- Paper plate

- Fabric painting medium for acrylic paint

- Gold metallic acrylic craft paint

- Rubber stamp with background design

- Cosmetic sponge

- Black velvet pigskin suede, 6" x 11" (15 x 28 cm)

- Black lining fabric, 4" x 5" (10 x 12.7 cm)

- Two black zippers, 7" (18 cm) long

- Black polyester thread

- Basting glue

- Leather needle for sewing machine

- Tear-away stabilizer, cut in $3/4$" (2 cm) strips

- Clear vinyl, 5" x $31/4$" (12.7 x 8.2 cm)

- Paper clips

- 2 yd. (1.85 m) black imitation leather cord, 2 mm wide

- 22 7-mm transparent gold glass beads

1. On a paper plate, mix fabric medium into gold metallic paint, following the manufacturer's directions. Apply the paint lightly to the rubber stamp, using a cosmetic sponge. Stamp the right side of the black suede. Repeat as necessary to cover the entire piece. Allow to dry.

2. Cut the stamped suede into the following pieces: 5" x 6$1/4$", 5" x 3", 5" x $3/4$", and four 1" x $3/8$" (12.7 x 15.7, 12.7 x 7.5, 12.7 x 2, and four 2.5 x 1 cm).

3. Center a 5" (12.7 cm) lining edge along the edge of a zipper, right sides together. Stitch the lining to the zipper with a scant $1/4$" (6 mm) seam. Press the lining away from the zipper.

4. Place the lining faceup on the work surface with the zipper at the top. Place another zipper below the first one, over the lining, so the zipper tape edges touch. Place the large suede rectangle over the top zipper with the suede edge about $1/8$" (3 mm) from the zipper teeth. Place the $3/4$" (2 cm) strip over the zipper tapes between the rows of teeth. Place the 5" x 3" piece over the bottom zipper, aligning the lower and side edges to the lining edges and the upper edge $1/8$" (3 mm) from the zipper teeth. Secure the suede pieces to the zipper tapes with basting glue.

5. Topstitch the large suede piece to the top zipper a scant $1/8$" (3 mm) from the suede edge, stitching over a strip of tear-away stabilizer. Topstitch the narrow strip to the other side of the same zipper in the same way. Take care not to catch the lining in the stitches. Tear away the stabilizer strips.

6. Fold the lining toward the top zipper. Topstitch the other edge of the narrow suede strip to the bottom zipper, stitching over a strip of tear-away stabilizer. Topstitch the lower suede piece in place in the same way. Tear away the stabilizer strips.

7. Fold the bag in half and mark the fold line at the edges; unfold. Fold the small strips in half, wrong sides together, and sparingly glue the ends together. Glue these tabs to the outer edges of the bag, aligning the glued ends to the bag edges, one on each side just below the fold line and one on each side $1/4$" (6 mm) from the bottom.

Continued on next page>

TIPS FOR SEWING LEATHER AND SUEDE:

- To remove wrinkles, press lightly from the wrong side, using a dry iron on medium setting and a dry press cloth.

- For precise cuts with smooth edges, use a rotary cutter and mat.

- Use a leather needle for machine sewing. It cuts a tiny slit rather than a round role.

- To prevent tearing, set the machine to a straight stitch of seven to 10 stitches per inch. Tie threads to secure them; never backstitch.

- Place strips of tear-away stabilizer over and under the leather to prevent drag when stitching.

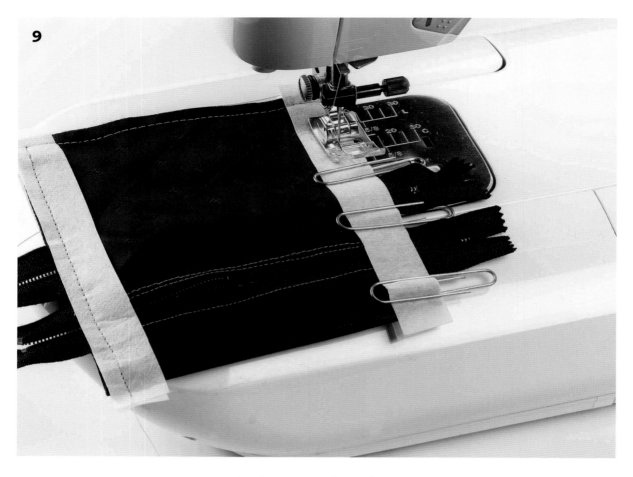

9

8. Open the zippers to the middle of the bag. Fold the bag in half, right sides together, aligning the suede edges and the lining edges. Insert the vinyl piece between the suede layers. Hold the layers together with paper clips.

9. Place tear-away stabilizer strips above and below the bag along the edges. Stitch

the three open sides with 1/4" (6 mm) seams. Tear away the stabilizer strips. Trim the zipper ends even with the bag edges. Trim the corners diagonally. Turn the bag right side out through the open zipper.

10. Cut two pieces of cord, 36" (91.5 cm) each. Tie an overhand knot in the end of one cord. String three beads and then run the cord

through a bottom tab. String two beads and tie an overhand knot snug against the top bead. Tie another overhand knot, leaving room for two beads below the upper tab. String two beads and run the cord through the upper tab. String three beads and tie an overhand knot snug against the top bead. Repeat with the other cord on the other side of the bag.

11. Following the diagram, tie the end of each cord onto the other cord in a tarbuck knot. This is a slide-and-grip knot that will make the length adjustable. Leave 6" (15 cm) tails.

12. Tie an overhand knot ¹/₂" (1.3 cm) from one tarbuck knot. String one bead. Tie an overhand knot snug against the bead, and cut the end. Repeat with the other cord end.

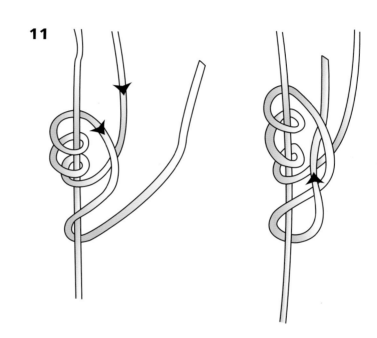

11

Retro Makeup Bag

JOANNE WAWRA AND TERESA HENN

Primp in style with a makeup bag inspired by the 1950s, when makeup was serious business. There are lots of retro fabrics to choose from. We picked bold pink dots on a black background for the outside, and black dots on pink for the inside. The lining is laminated with vinyl so it will wipe clean. Check out the fun pompom on the zipper pull!

what SIZZLES

Retro fabrics like polka dots

Fun pompom detail

1. Apply iron-on vinyl to the right side of the lining, covering an area about 9" x 16" (23 x 40.5 cm), following the manufacturer's directions. Allow the fabric to cool. Cut the lining 8¹/₂" x 15" (21.8 x 38 cm).

2. Using the lining as a pattern, cut a rectangle of outer fabric.

3. Pin a closed zipper, face-down, to the right side of the outer fabric, aligning the zipper tape edge to one narrow raw edge of the fabric. The ends of the zipper will extend beyond the fabric. Stitch ¹/₄" (6 mm) from the edge, using a zipper foot.

4. Align the opposite narrow end of the bag to the other side of the zipper, right sides together, and stitch as in step 3.

5. Open the zipper. Place the lining and outer bag right sides together along one narrow edge, sandwiching the zipper between them. With the wrong side of the outer bag facing up, stitch over the previous stitches. Repeat at the opposite end.

you will need

- Therm O Web iron-on vinyl (one roll)
- ³/₈ yd. (0.35 m) lining
- ³/₈ yd. (0.35 m) outer fabric
- 12" (30.5 cm) conventional zipper
- Zipper foot
- Cotton yarn
- Pompom maker
- Ruler
- Scissors

6. Close the zipper partially. Pin the side seams together, with lining to lining and outer bag to outer bag. Match the zipper seamlines, and turn the zipper teeth toward the outer bag. Stitch ¹/₄" (6 mm) seams, leaving a 3" (7.5 cm) opening in the lining on one side. Stitch carefully over the zipper teeth.

7. Cut off the ends of the zipper. Open the zipper and turn the bag and lining right side out. Turn in the seam allowances of the opening and topstitch closed.

8. Push the outer bag into the lining, aligning the seams and corners. Flatten one lower corner into a triangle with the seamline in the center. Mark a line 2" (5 cm) from the corner perpendicular to the seam. Stitch on the line. Repeat for the opposite corner.

9. Turn the bag right side out. Make the pompom, following the manufacturer's directions.

Amulet Pouch

LINDA NEUBAUER AND CAROL PILOT

An amulet pouch holds something that's small but special. It is quick to sew and fun to personalize, and makes a great present. This design recycles the beautiful silk fabric of a vintage tie. Embellished with beads, it is practically jewelry. What you choose to hide inside will be your little secret.

what
SIZZLES

Amulet pouches

Recycling a great tie

Bead embellishments

Amulet Template

you will need

- Stiff card or template plastic

- Silk necktie, at least 3$\frac{1}{4}$" (8.2 cm) at the widest point

- 11 pony beads

- Beads and sequins

- Beading needle

- Thread

- 1$\frac{1}{4}$ yd. (1.15 m) cord

1. Trace the pattern and cut a template from stiff card or template plastic. Cut off the wide end of the necktie to the template length. Remove any stitches holding the center edges together.

2. Remove the interfacing and recut it, using the template as a guide. Reinsert the interfacing into the center of the tie.

3. Insert the template into the tie and press the sides toward the center along the template edges. Hand-stitch the center edges together where they meet. Remove the template.

4. Turn the tie inside out. Stitch a 1/4" (6 mm) seam across the straight end through all layers.

5. Turn the tie right side out. Press. Slipstitch the diagonal edges on the back of the tie to the lining.

6. Place the tie wrong side up. Fold the bottom up 3" (7.5 cm). Fold the top flap down so the point is near the lower edge. Press lightly.

7. Open the flap. Hand-stitch the sides together, leaving 1/4" (6 mm) openings at the bottom fold for inserting the cord.

8. Stitch five pony beads, evenly spaced, to each side of the pouch, with the holes aligned vertically. Place the top beads even with the top fold line; place the bottom beads just above the opening.

9. Thread the cord ends down through the pony beads and into the bottom openings. Adjust the length. Tie the ends together, hiding the knot inside the pouch.

10. Stitch sequins and beads to the front flap as desired, highlighting the design of the fabric. Stitch a pony bead to the center of the lower fold. Stitch a thread loop to the point of the flap for the closure.

5

9

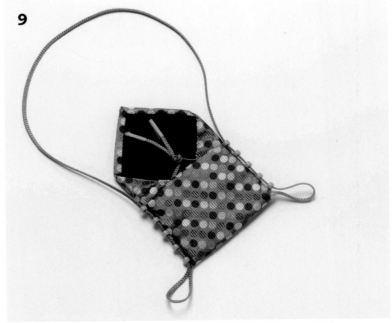

Floral Flair

DENISE GILES

Big roses are blooming everywhere: lapels, sweaters, chokers, hats, hand-bags. It's easy to create your own with satin, wired-edge ribbon. A rosebud and leaves peeking out from under the rose petals provide the perfect finishing touch. This is a deluxe, realistic rose that will add color and class to everything from a suit to an evening bag. Pin it on your jean jacket for a funky look.

what
SIZZLES

Big blooming flowers

Personalizing the look with the ribbon you choose

you will need

- 2²/₃ yd. (2.48 m) of wired-edge ribbon for rose, 1¹/₂" (39 mm) wide

- 21" (53.5 cm) of wired-edge green ombre ribbon for leaves, 1¹/₂" (39 mm) wide

- Hand needle

- Sewing thread

- Fabric glue

- 3" (7.5 cm) square of ivory felt

- Pin backing

1. Thread a hand needle; set aside. Cut 16" (40.5 cm) of pink ribbon for the rose center. Fold one end under diagonally. Beginning at the folded end, roll the ribbon, keeping the upper edge of the roll along the fold. This will form the rose center. Roll two or three times until you near the end of the fold. Hand-tack the layers together at the lower edge.

2. Just before the end of the first fold, fold the ribbon back diagonally again and continue rolling the rose center, keeping the upper edge along the fold. When you near the end of the second fold, hand-tack the lower edge. Continue folding, rolling, and tacking to the end of the ribbon to form a rosette about 1¹/₄" (3.2 cm) in diameter.

3. Cut three 5" (12.7 cm) pieces and five 7" (18 cm) pieces of pink ribbon for the rose petals. With needle and thread, stitch a continuous running stitch across one short edge, along one long edge, and across the other short edge of each piece. Pull the thread to gather the ribbon, forming a petal. Secure the thread.

4. Glue the three small petals around the rosette center, slightly overlapping them. Overlap and glue the rest of the petals on the outer edge to form the rose.

5. Cut 8" (20.5 cm) of pink ribbon for the rose bud. Shape the bud into a rosette as in steps 1 and 2.

6. Cut 5" (12.7 cm) of green ribbon. Wrap the ribbon around the bud, crossing the ends of the ribbon in the front. Tack with glue and twist the ribbon ends together.

2

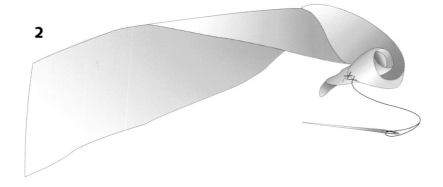

4

7

7. Cut two 8" (20.5 cm) pieces of green ribbon for the leaves. Fold the ribbon in half crosswise. Fold the dark corners down diagonally. Stitch a continuous running stitch from one point, along the diagonal fold, along the dark edges, and along the other fold to the other point. Pull the thread to gather the ribbon until the stitched line lays straight. Secure the thread. Open the ribbon to form the leaf.

8. Glue the bud and leaves in place behind the large rose.

9. Cut the felt in a large circle to fit the back of the rose and cover raw edges. Center the pin backing on the felt and mark the felt even with the pin ends. Cut two slits in the felt at the marks. Open the pin. Slip the ends through the slits from the back of the felt. Glue the felt to the back of the rose.

Cinched Suede Belt

PATRICIA CONVERSE

Cinch your waist or hips with suede. Pull snug and tie once. Suede is flexible, so it's comfortable to wear. The belt is accented with a beaded suede flower; it slips over the belt, so you can make a couple to match different outfits. You'll find tips for sewing on leather and suede on page 61.

what
SIZZLES

Soft, supple suede

Putting the accent on your waist or hips with a beaded flower

you will need

- White velvet pigskin suede, 12" (30.5 cm) square

- Zig Painty paint markers with medium tips, in yellow and pink

- Polyester thread to match belt, flower, and beads

- 15 4-mm yellow glass beads

- Forest green velvet pigskin suede, amount determined in step 6

- Leather sewing machine needle

- Basting glue

- Tear-away stabilizer

- Pinking shears

1. Trace the flower patterns (page 81); cut out. Trace the patterns lightly onto the wrong side of the suede, using a pencil. Cut out the flower parts.

2. Add color to the flower parts with markers, working from the center outward with a light motion. Use yellow near the center and blend into pink for the outer petals.

3. Thread a hand-sewing needle with a double strand of white thread. Hand-stitch with a running stitch around the center of a petal section; leave long thread tails at the beginning and end, on the wrong side. Pull the thread tails taut to gather the petal section, and knot securely on the wrong side. Trim threads. Repeat for each petal section.

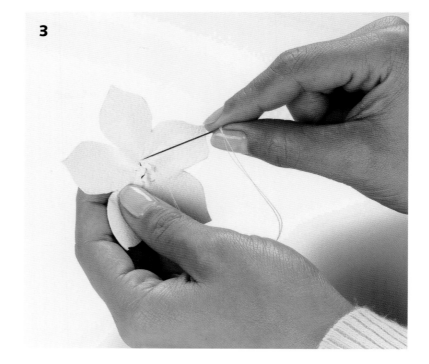

3

5

4. Thread a hand-sewing needle with a double strand of yellow thread. Stack the petal layers. Insert the needle through the petal centers from the back, leaving a long tail on the flower back. String three beads, and return the needle to the flower back. Pull snug and tie, but do not cut the threads. Repeat four more times to make the beaded stamens. Trim after the last knot.

5. Cut a 1" x 3" (2.5 x 7.5 cm) white suede strip. Fold the strip into thirds length-wise. Stitch down the center. Overlap the ends forming a loop; hand-stitch. Tack the loop to the back of the flower.

6. Measure the waist and add 12" (30.5 cm); divide by 2 to determine the length to cut the belt pieces. Cut four pieces of green suede 2^1/$_2$" (6.5 cm) wide by this length. Overlap two ends ^{1}/$_4$" (6 mm), and topstitch them together ^{1}/$_8$" (3 mm) from one edge, for the belt front. Repeat with the other two pieces for the belt back.

Continued on next page>

Belt End Template

7. Trace the belt end template; cut out. Trace the template onto the wrong side of each end of the belt front and back. Cut on the marked lines.

8. Glue-baste the belt front and back, wrong sides together. Cut two strips of tear-away stabilizer, using the belt as a guide for length. Sandwich the belt between them. Using green thread, topstitch around the entire belt $1/4$" (6 mm) from the edge. Tear away the stabilizer. Knot the threads and bury the tails between the layers.

9. Fancy-cut the outer edge of the belt carefully, using pinking shears.

Flower Patterns

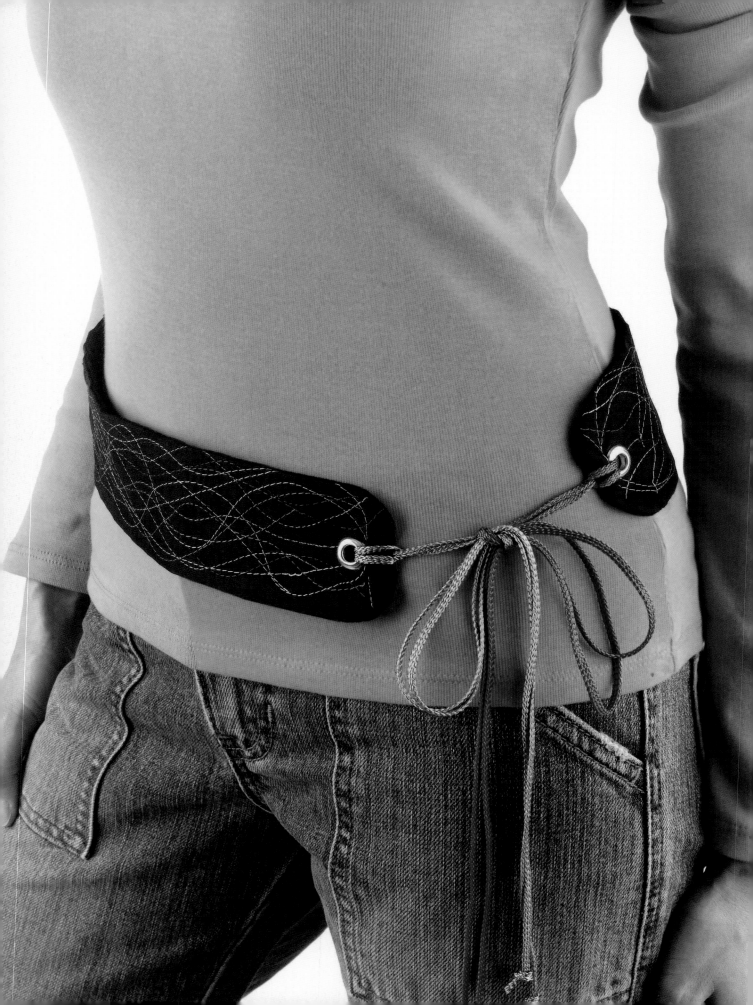

Thread Trails Sash

JOANNE WAWRA AND CAROL PILOT

This fascinating belt is embellished with bright, meandering threads and tied with streamers. Wear it over anything from a fancy dress to your favorite jeans. Variegated rayon threads are stitched on black silk. The sash is easy to make in any size and can be worn at the waist or hips. Plan for a gap of about 3" (7.5 cm) between the sash ends when the cords are tied.

you will need

- 1/4 yd. (0.25 m) sash fabric

- 1/4 yd. (0.25 m) light-weight, fusible interfacing

- Marking chalk

- Various colors of varie-gated thread

- Two grommets and attaching tool

- 1 1/2 yd. (1.4 m) each of flat braids in two colors

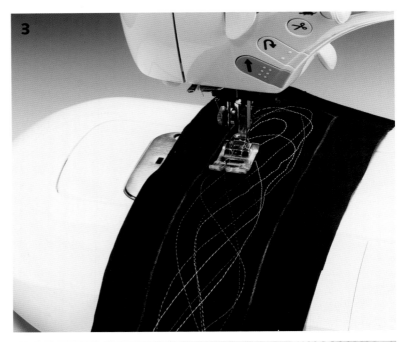

1. Determine the desired length of the sash. Cut a strip of fabric 4" (10 cm) wide and 2" (5 cm) longer than the desired sash size. Cut interfacing to the same size and fuse it to the wrong side of the sash fabric.

2. Mark the outline of the finished sash on the right side of the fabric strip, using chalk; round the ends.

3. Stitch gently waving lines up and down the length of the strip within the chalked area, using various colors of variegated thread. Pull all thread tails to the back and knot them.

4. Trim the sash $1/2$" (1.3 cm) beyond the marked line. Cut a sash facing, using the sash front as a pattern.

5. Pin the facing to the sash front, right sides together. Stitch a $1/2$" (1.3 cm) seam, leaving a 3" (7.5 cm) opening along one side. Trim the curves and corners and grade the seam allowances.

6. Turn the sash right side out and press. Turn the seam allowances to the inside at the opening and slipstitch in place.

7. Attach grommets $1/2$" (1.3 cm) from the sash ends, following the manufacturer's directions.

8. Knot the ends of the braids. Fold one braid in half and insert the fold through the grommet from the back. Slip the braid ends through the loop and pull snug. Repeat at the other end with the other braid.

Scarves & Wraps

Beaded Highlights Scarf

LINDA NEUBAUER

So many fabrics would make wonderful scarves. Sew them up in any size and shape you like to wear. Look for fabrics that look good on both sides. For example, this cotton print (found at a quilt shop) is saturated with dyes straight through the fabric. A narrow, mitered, double-fold hem finishes the edge nicely and is done in minutes.

Add a touch of beaded flair. If the fabric has a pattern or motif, simply outline a design for an instant focal point.

you will need

- ³/₄ yd. (0.7 m) fabric
- Thread
- Beads in various colors, shapes, and sizes
- Beading needle

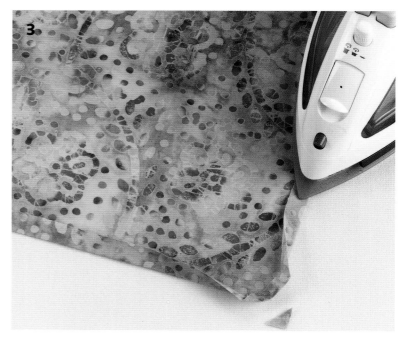

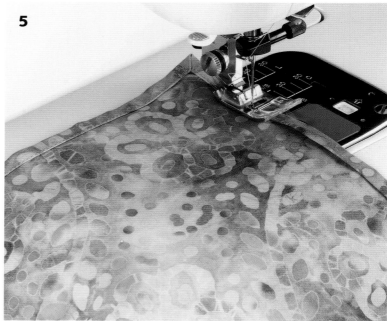

1. Cut the scarf 1" (2.5 cm) wider and longer than the desired finished size, centering a full design motif near one corner. If possible, plan the size of the scarf to allow a full design motif near each corner.

2. Turn under ¹/₂" (2.5 cm) on all edges and press.

3. Open a corner. Fold the corner in diagonally so the pressed folds align; press the diagonal fold. Trim off the corner diagonally at the inner foldlines. Repeat at each corner.

4. Fold under the raw edge ¹/₄" (6 mm), so the raw edge meets the foldline. Then fold again on the first foldline and press.

5. Stitch as close as possible to the inner fold. Pivot with the needle down in the fabric at the corners.

6. Hand-stitch beads to one or all corner motifs to highlight colors and design elements. Use a backstitch to secure beads in a continuous line. Use a stop stitch to attach larger beads. Stitch dangles at the corners, if desired.

Backstitch: Bring the needle up through three seed beads; slide the beads down the thread to the fabric surface. Insert the needle back through the fabric at the end of the third bead. Bring the needle back up through the fabric between the first and second beads, running the needle also through the second and third beads.

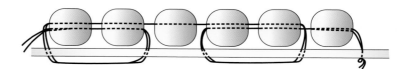

Stop stitch: Bring the needle up through the large bead and a seed bead on the right side of the fabric. (The seed bead is called the "stop.") Bring the needle back through the large bead, then down through the fabric to the wrong side, and secure the thread.

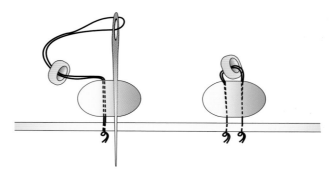

Dangles: Bring the needle up through several beads on the right side of the fabric; the last bead, or stop, is usually a small seed bead. Bring the needle back through all the beads except the stop bead, then down through the fabric to the wrong side. Knot the thread on the wrong side after each dangle stitch.

Gossamer Scarf

DIANE BARTELS

This fascinating, whisper-light scarf looks woven, but is actually sewn together. Raw, hand-dyed fibers called "top" are held together with nothing but a grid of stitches. Top is fibers of silk, viscose, tencel, wool, or synthetics that have been cleaned and carded, but not yet spun into thread or yarn. It is available in most weaving or spinning stores and from Internet sources. For even more surface texture, you can add yarns, decorative threads, snips of cloth, or ribbons.

what
SIZZLES

Making a textile scarf without knowing how to knit or weave

Fascinating hand-dyed colors

Free-form stitching

you will need

- 12" x 70" (30.5 x 178 cm) water-soluble stabilizer, such as Super Solvy or Ultra Solvy

- 1/2 oz. hand-dyed top in desired colors

- Temporary spray adhesive

- Large spool of multicolored thread

- Straight pins with colored heads

- Sewing machine

- Walking foot, optional

- Water

- Towel

1. Cut the stabilizer in half lengthwise, so you have two 6" x 70" (15 x 178 cm) strips. Place one strip of stabilizer flat on the work surface. Lay teased fluffs of top randomly over the stabilizer to within 1" (2.5 cm) of the edges. Vary the colors and density of the top. Add snippets of cloth or other yarns and threads, if desired.

2. Mist the scarf lightly with temporary spray adhesive. Touch a moistened finger to several areas in the outer margin of the stabilizer. Place the other stabilizer strip over the fibers, aligning the stabilizer edges. Pat with your hands so the layers stick together. Pin the layers together here and there as necessary.

3. Thread the sewing machine with multicolored thread. Attach a walking foot, if you have one. Stitch around the outer edge of the scarf to anchor the layers. Then stitch irregular crosswise lines from one side to the other, spacing them about 1/2" (1.3 cm) apart. At the sides, pivot on or just after the outer stitching line, and stitch the next line.

4. Stitch irregular lengthwise lines about 1/2" (1.3 cm) apart over the entire scarf. Make sure to pivot on or outside of the outer stitching line. If desired, add free-motion stitches.

5. Soak the scarf in water for about 20 minutes or until the stabilizer is completely dissolved. Gently remove the scarf from the water and rinse it in clear water. Roll the scarf in a towel to remove excess water. Lay the scarf flat to dry.

1

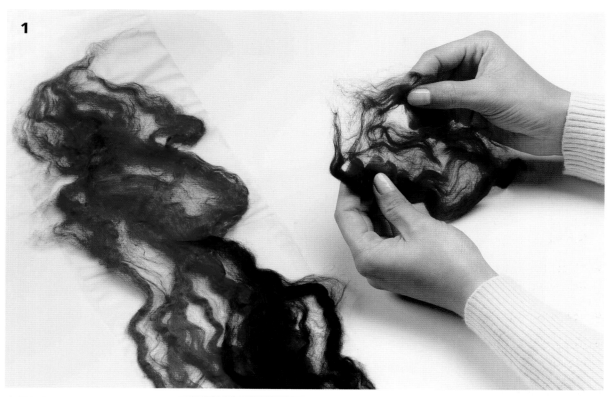

3

Primo Painted Scarf

ELAINE JACKSON

This scarf is as hot as the tropics. Hand-painted scarves are very elegant, but most silk dyes are a hassle. Instead, paint with Dye-na-flow colors, a product that produces rich colors, leaves fabrics supple, and doesn't need to be set with a complicated steam process.

what
SIZZLES

Hand-painted fabric

Tropical colors
and motifs

- Rubber gloves

- Yellow and fuchsia Rit liquid dyes

- Large, flat plastic container for dyeing

- Measuring spoons

- $3/8$ yd. (0.35 m) white rayon fabric, 60" (152.5 cm) wide

- Wooden spoon

- Small plastic container

- Pencil

- Masking tape

- Wooden frame stretcher bars, two 24" (61 cm) and two 14" (35.5 cm)

- Water-based resist and applicator

- Dye-na-flow paints in the following colors: sun yellow, golden yellow, bright orange, magenta, brilliant red, chartreuse, and emerald green

- Paintbrush

- Small container for mixing paints

- Superclear dye thickener

1. Put on rubber gloves. Prepare a yellow dye bath in the large, flat plastic container, using two teaspoons of yellow dye and hot water poured to about 1" (2.5 cm) deep. Place the fabric into the dye bath in a single, rumpled layer. Allow the fabric to soak for 15 to 20 minutes, occasionally shifting the fabric around with a wooden spoon. Remove the fabric from the dye bath and wring out excess dye.

2. Prepare a fuchsia dye bath in a small container. Dip the scarf ends into the dye, allowing the color to spread up into the scarf 3" to 4" (7.5 to 10 cm). Remove from dye. Rinse in cold water until water runs clear. Allow to air dry.

3. Make several copies of the flower design (page 101) and arrange them on the work surface; tape in place. Place the scarf over the designs and trace with a pencil. Draw freehand stems and leaves in empty areas.

4. Apply masking tape around the outer edges of the fabric. Tape the fabric taut to a stretcher-bar frame, allowing excess fabric to hang off one end.

5. Fill the applicator with water-based resist. Apply resist over the design in steady, consistent lines. Begin at one end and avoid touching areas with wet resist. If you are right-handed, work from left to right. If you are left-handed, work from right to left. Allow the resist to dry. Then reposition the fabric on the frame to complete the other half.

5

Continued on next page>

6. Keep the fabric taped taut to the frame. Apply sun yellow dye to the flower centers. Dip the tip of the paintbrush into the dye; touch the brush to the center of the desired area. Allow the dye to transfer from the brush to the fabric and spread toward the resist. Ease the dye toward the outer edges of the area as necessary, using the brush tip.

7. Before the dye dries, shade the left side of each line with orange.

8. Apply magenta dye to the outer areas of each flower, as in step 6. Shade with bright red, as in step 7. Apply chartreuse to the leaves and shade with emerald green.

9. In a small container, mix small amounts of chartreuse and emerald green to the desired leaf color. Add thickener until the mixture resembles a creamy paste. Paint the hand-drawn stems and leaves. Allow the fabric to dry.

10. Remove the fabric from the frame. Heat-set the designs by pressing with dry heat from the wrong side for at least three minutes, follow the manufacturer's directions.

11. Cut the scarf to 12" x 56" (30.5 x 142 cm). Finish the edges with $1/4$" (6 mm) double-fold hems.

Flower Design

Scarf of Many Colors

JOANNE WAWRA AND TERESA HENN

This dramatic scarf is a continuum of fabrics in different colors, patterns, and textures, all pieced together. You could use scraps from previous sewing projects, or check out the fabric store's remnant bins for small pieces too inviting to pass up. For a splashy finishing touch, trim the scarf ends with beaded fringe.

what
SIZZLES

Mixing and matching
colors and textures

Beaded fringe

Taking one scarf on
a trip, knowing it'll
go with everything

1. Cut eight rectangles (one of each fabric) 7" to 9" (18 to 23 cm) long and 14½" (36.8 cm) wide. Arrange the pieces in a pleasing order.

2. Sew the rectangles together on the long edges, using ¼" (6 mm) seam allowances. Finish raw edges that ravel easily. Press the seam allowances toward the scarf center.

3. Mark the centers of the short ends with pins. Cut two strips of beaded fringe, each 7" (18 cm) long. Pin the fringe to the right side of the scarf ends, from the center to ¼" (6 mm) from the outer edge, aligning the top of the fringe heading to the raw edge of the scarf. Baste as close as possible to the beaded edge, using a zipper foot.

4. Fold the scarf in half lengthwise, right sides together, aligning seams. Pin through each of the aligned seams. Stitch the long edge and both ends, leaving a 4" (10 cm) opening in the long edge for turning. Stitch carefully over the basting stitching in the ends, using a zipper foot.

5. Turn the scarf right side out through the opening. Press lightly. Slipstitch the opening closed.

2

3

Magic Boa

LINDA NEUBAUER

This is a very snuggly boa. It's made from layers of fabric. You stitch them together in channels, slash them, and fluff—magic! For the best results, use a multicolor rayon print fabric in which the dyes have saturated through to the back. Very light wools also work well. The fabric's design will get lost, so the colors are the most important consideration when picking.

what
SIZZLES

Fanciful, fun look

Soft and cuddly
to wear

Telling your friends
how you made this!

4

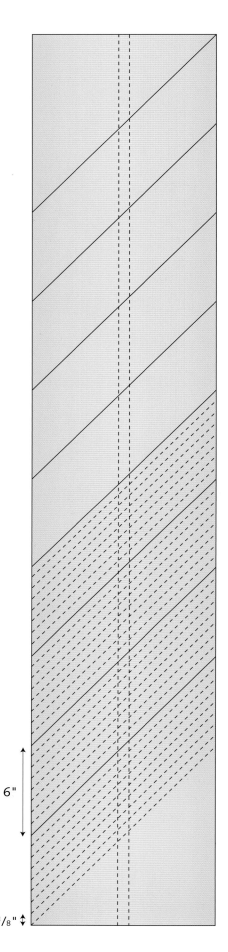

6"

³/₈"

1. Square the cut ends of the fabric by pulling a thread and cutting along the line left by the pulled thread. Fold the fabric in half crosswise; press the fold. Repeat twice, forming eight even layers.

2. Mark 45-degree lines across the top layer every 6" (15 cm), using a removable fabric marker. Mark another line down the center. Secure the layers together with quilter's safety pins spaced about 6" (15 cm) apart.

3. Set the machine to stitch a 2 mm straight stitch. Attach a walking foot. Stitch the layers together down the center, stitching 1/4" (6 mm) on each side of the marked line.

4. Beginning near the center, stitch across the layers on a diagonal line. Then turn the fabric around and stitch back 3/8" (1 cm) from the first line. Continue stitching diagonal lines 3/8" (1 cm) apart until one end of the stitching line reaches the narrow end of the layers. Then stitch diagonal lines from the center to the opposite end. Use the marked lines to check that the stitching lines are kept at 45-degree angles.

5. Trim away the ends 3/16" (4.5 mm) from the last stitching lines. Trim off the folds on the long edges.

6. Slash the layers from the long edges to within 1/8" (3 mm) of the center stitching lines, cutting halfway between the diagonal stitching lines. Use shears or a rotary cutter.

7. Machine-wash in cool water with average agitation for 10 minutes. Tumble dry. The layers will separate and the fibers will fluff. The individual strands of the boa will spiral. Stop the dryer and disentangle strands periodically as necessary.

5

6

Bleached Beach Wrap

ELAINE JACKSON

Look sensational in this colorful beach wrap, also called a pareu, sarong, toga, or kanga. Any way you tie this wrap, it sizzles! It's made by piecing together strips of rayon. Each strip is hand-dyed and then creatively patterned using ordinary bleach and a bleach pen (the technical name of the process is "discharge dyeing"). See page 128 for sources of white rayon. If you don't want to dye the fabric, choose bright rayons in solid colors.

See page 128 for sources of white rayon.

what SIZZLES

Bleached-out designs

Bright dyes

All the ways you can wear it

- 1 3/8 yd. (1.3 m) white rayon, 60" (152.5 cm) wide

- Rubber gloves

- Fabric dyes in five colors

- Small plastic containers for dyeing

- Wooden spoons

- Plastic sheeting

- Tape

- Comet bleach cream

- Chunky foam stamps

- Foam applicator

- Clorox bleach pen

- Bleach-Stop or antichlor

1. Tear the rayon on the crosswise grain into five 8" (20.5 cm) strips. Put on rubber gloves. Prepare separate dye baths for the strips in small plastic containers, and dye strips as in step 1 on page 98. Rinse each strip separately in cold water until the water runs clear. Allow to air dry. Press.

2. Protect the work surface with plastic sheeting. Tape a dyed rayon strip to the plastic.

3. Apply a thin layer of bleach cream to a chunky foam stamp, using a foam applicator. Stamp the fabric. Repeat for each design. Allow the bleach to work for several minutes.

4. Apply lines of bleach to the fabric, using a bleach pen. Allow the bleach to work for several minutes.

5. Rinse the bleach away and agitate the discharged pieces in a solution of Bleach-Stop (sodium thiosulfate, also called antichlor) and warm water, according to the manufacturer's directions. This will stop the action of the bleach. Allow to air dry.

6. Sew the strips together in French seams. Press all the seams toward the lower edge.

7. Finish the outer edges in 1/4" (6 mm) double-fold hems.

HOW TO WEAR A BEACH WRAP:

- To wear it like a skirt, tie it at two upper corners around your waist, putting the tie at the side or center.

- To wear it as a dress, bring the upper edge up under your arms and tie the corners in the center, or twist the ends and tie them behind your neck.

- Tie the upper corners in a small knot, give them a half twist to form a loop, and slip your arm through the loop so the knot rests on your shoulder and the upper edge circles your upper chest.

3

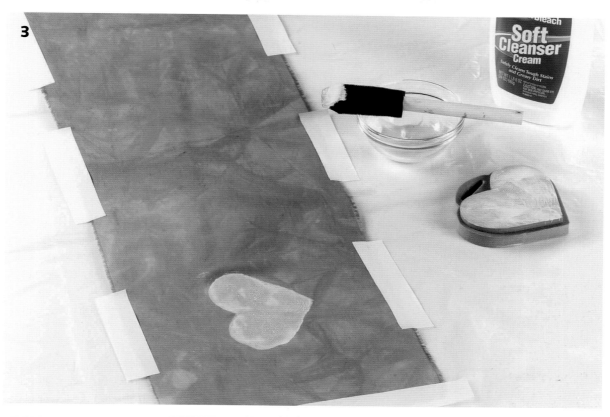

4

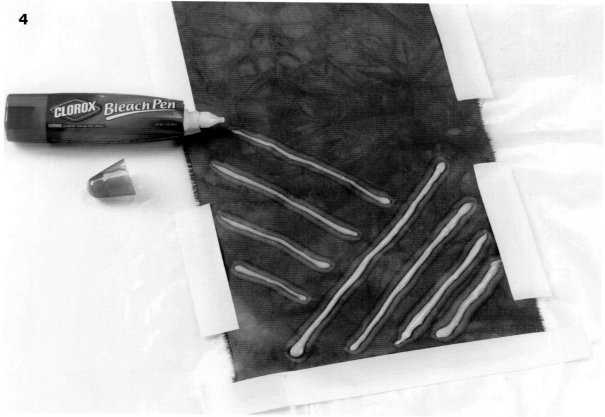

Spicy Sheer Wrap

JOANNE WAWRA AND TERESA HENN

Wrap your shoulders in sheer elegance. Fabulous organza is the fabric, decorated with textured yarns using a technique called couching. Take your fabric along when you shop for yarn and experiment with all the incredible choices that are available.

Sheer organza can be difficult to cut in a straight line, but it can be easily torn along the grain. A simple rolled, zigzagged hem, sewn on a conventional machine, is used to finish the edges. When couching the yarn onto the organza, don't be concerned about straight lines or consistently spaced or sized loops. Variety only adds more spice!

what SIZZLES

Lively loops of textured yarn

Delightfully sheer and provocative look

1. Tear the organza across the ends to straighten them. Then tear the wrap along both lengthwise edges to the desired width. The wrap shown is about 30" (76 cm) wide.

2. Attach the open toe embroidery presser foot and thread the machine with embroidery thread. Set the machine for a stitch width of 4 mm and a stitch length of 2 mm. Holding the fabric taut in front of the presser foot, stitch, guiding the fabric edge just to the right of the center of the foot. The right swing of the needle will roll the fabric edge as the machine zigzags over it.

3. Set the machine for a straight stitch. Place the wrap under the presser foot, 4" (10 cm) from the end. Center the yarn under the presser foot, leaving a 4" (10 cm) tail behind the presser foot. Backstitch to secure.

4. Stitch forward, stitching through the center of the yarn. Use the finished edge of the wrap as a general guide. Lines of yarn need not be perfectly straight. At the desired point for the first loop, stop with the needle down in the fabric, and raise the presser foot. Using the crochet hook, pull a loop of yarn from under the foot, and move it to the back of the foot. Lower the presser foot and resume stitching.

5. Continue stitching and making loops, spacing them as desired. Backstitch to secure 4" (10 cm) from the opposite end. Remove the fabric from the machine. Cut the yarn, leaving a 4" (10 cm) tail.

6. Repeat steps 4 and 5, spacing the rows as desired.

7. Pull out the crosswise threads in the last $3^3/4$" (9.5 cm) of the ends. Beginning at one side, twist together the lengthwise threads in the first $1/2$" (1.3 cm), and tie a knot at the top. Seal the knot with a drop of liquid fray preventer. Repeat across to fringe the entire end. Then fringe the opposite end.

2

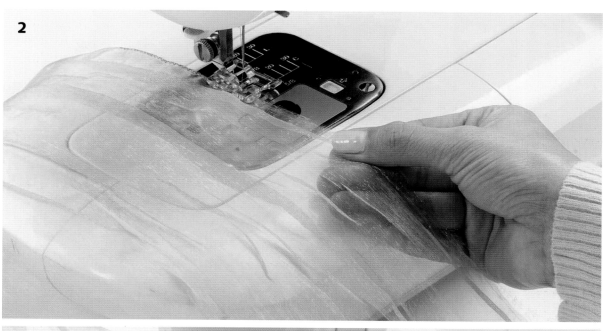

4

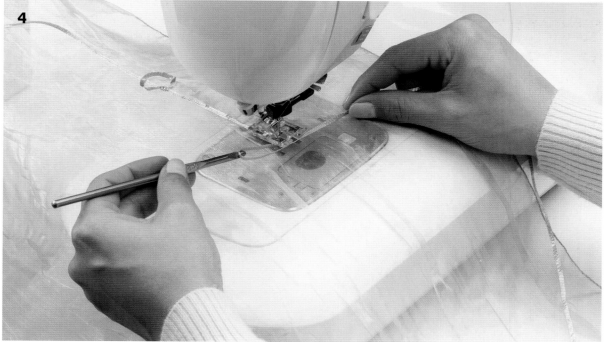

Fur Capelet

CAROL ZENTGRAF

Wrap yourself in luxury with a faux fur capelet. This loose-fitting shoulder wrap is so quick and easy that you may want to make several in different fur colors. It's fully lined and closes with a luxurious bow. When you select the faux fur, go for the good stuff, with a thick pile and a silky feel. Lightly rub it to make sure it doesn't shed excessively. To care for your faux fur capelet, wash it in cold water. Air dry or dry it in a dryer set on a fluff cycle without heat.

1

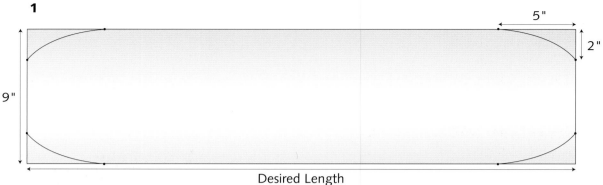

5"

2"

9"

Desired Length

1. Measure around your shoulders at the position for the capelet. On the wrong side of the fur, mark a rectangle that is this length and 9" (23 cm) wide, using a white dressmaker's pencil and a long quilter's ruler or straightedge. Mark points 5" (12.7 cm) from each corner on the long edges and 2" (5 cm) from each corner on the short edges. Draw curved lines to connect the marks at each corner. Note that after sewing the seams, there will be a short gap between the ends to allow for tying.

2. Cut out the capelet on the marked line. Cut through the backing only, being careful not to cut the fur nap.

2

3. Mark an identical rectangle with curved ends on the charmeuse, using a dressmaker's pencil. Cut out the fabric.

4. Cut two 8" x 34" (20.5 x 86.5 cm) strips for the ties. Fold each strip in half lengthwise, right sides together. Sew together along the long edges and one short edge using a $^{1}/_{2}$" (1.3 cm) seam allowance. Trim the corners, turn right side out, and press.

5. Pin the ties to the center of the capelet ends on the right side of the fur. Make sure the fur nap is running downward and the seams are along the lower edges of the ties. Pin. Baste in place. Roll each tie up and pin in place to prevent it from getting caught in the lining seam.

6. With right sides together and edges even, pin the lining to the fur. Pin closely, tucking in any fur that sticks out.

7. Sew the edges together, using a $^{1}/_{2}$" (1.3 cm) seam allowance and leaving a 6" (15 cm) opening in the lower edge for turning. Turn right side out and slipstitch the opening closed. Use the tapestry needle to pull out any fur that is caught in the seam.

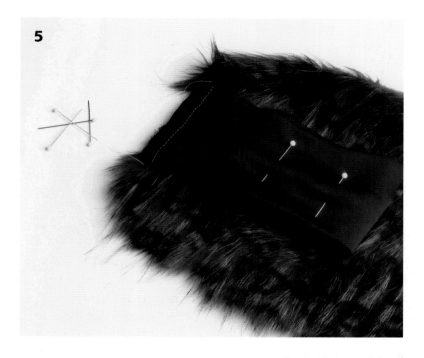

5

TIPS FOR SEWING FUR:

- Cut through the backing only, one layer at a time, without cutting the pile.

- Use long pins to pin layers together or to pin fur to lining. Pin closely, tucking the fur away from the seam.

- Use a size 80 or 90 universal needle and a roller foot or standard presser foot.

- Slightly reduce the presser foot pressure so the fabric moves smoothly when you stitch.

Diva's Velvet Cape

CAROL ZENTGRAF

Wrap yourself in this dreamy velvet cape dressed up with embossing and fringe. You can buy velvet and a matching trim, or get endless color choices by dyeing them yourself. White silk-back velvet with a rayon pile is ideal for dyeing as well as embossing, and white rayon fringe accepts the dye beautifully. See page 128 for sources of silk/rayon velvet. For heat embossing, choose a rubber stamp with a simple, deeply carved motif on a wooden base. To clean your embossed velvet cape, dry-clean without steam pressing, which would remove the embossed images.

you will need

- Rubber gloves

- Powdered fabric dye

- Large pot or sink

- 1 2/3 yd. (1.58 m) white silk/rayon velvet, 45" (115 cm) wide

- 3 yd. (2.75 m) rayon fringe, 6" (15 cm) long

- Wooden spoon

- Thick terrycloth towels

- Long quilter's ruler or straightedge

- Fabric marking pen

- Sharp scissors or a rotary cutter and mat

- Rubber stamp

- Spray bottle of water

- Iron

- Self-adhesive, double-sided basting tape

1. Mix the dye with hot water in a large pot or sink, following the manufacturer's instructions. If you are mixing two or more colors, dilute the lightest color first, then gradually add the darker colors, testing the color on a scrap of white fabric periodically until you achieve the desired color.

2. Dip the fabric and trim into the dye bath, stirring with a wooden spoon to distribute the dye evenly. When the desired color is reached, remove the fabric and trim from the dye bath.

3. Rinse the fabric and trim in cold water until the water runs clear.

4. Machine dry the velvet and trim on a delicate setting or air dry. The fringe ends will fray when dried in the dryer.

5. Place the velvet face-down over thick terrycloth towels and press lightly, using an iron set on silk setting. Steam the fringe to straighten it as much as desired.

6. To cut the triangle shape from the velvet, fold the fabric in half crosswise, right sides together. Mark a point 29" (73.5 cm) from the fold along the selvages on one side. Mark another point on the fold 36" (91.5 cm) from the same selvages. Draw a straight line to connect the marks. Cut along the line through both layers using sharp scissors or a rotary cutter, quilter's ruler, and mat.

6

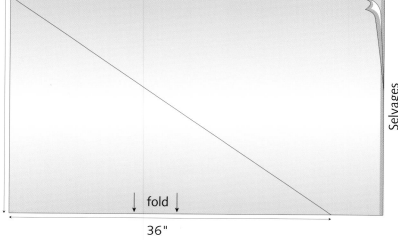

29"

fold

36"

Selvages

7. To emboss the velvet, place the stamp right side up on an ironing board or other heat-resistant surface. Position the velvet face-down over the stamp and lightly mist the wrong side with water. Use a dry iron set on medium heat to firmly press the velvet on the stamp for 20 seconds. Do not slide the iron while pressing, and avoid letting the steam holes touch the fabric.

8. Lift the iron straight up. Let the fabric cool before removing it from the stamp. Repeat to emboss random motifs on the velvet triangle, alternating the direction of the motifs as you work.

9. Adhere a strip of basting tape to the cut edges on the right side of the triangle. Remove the paper backing from the tape. Adhere the fringe heading to the cape edges. Begin and end the trim 1" (2.5 cm) from the straight edge.

10. Turn the fringe heading to the wrong side of the fabric. Topstitch in place from the right side of the fabric, stitching close to the edge of the heading.

11. Turn under the straight edge $1/2$" (1.3 cm) and adhere with basting tape. Turn under $1/2$" (1.3 cm) again and topstitch $3/8$" (1 cm) from the edge.

Accessory Designers

DIANE BARTELS dyes and prints fabrics, yarns, and fibers in her home studio in Mound, Minnesota. She uses a wide range of printing techniques in her textile art: screen printing, sun printing, stamping, stenciling, and high-tech computer processes.

PATRICIA CONVERSE is an artist, crafter, and avid quilter. Her designs are inspired by the natural setting of her rural Pennsylvania home. A member of the Society of Creative Designers, Pat is also an author and teacher, with a degree in home economics.

DENISE GILES is an author, designer, teacher, demonstrator, and needlework and ribbon artist. Hundreds of her designs have been published in books and magazines. She has been a member of the Society of Creative Designers since 1998.

TERESA HENN has been a sewing and craft enthusiast for most of her life. She has worked for a major sewing machine company and has designed many projects for book and magazine publishers.

ELAINE JACKSON studied fashion design and pattern making at the Fashion Institute of Design and Merchandising in Los Angeles. Her design experience includes rubber stamps, patterns for needlepoint canvases and embroidery, clothing, and surface design. Elaine shows more of her work on her web site: http://www.home.earthlink.net/~bird-and-flower

LINDA NEUBAUER is the senior editor for the Lifestyles department of Creative Publishing. A lifelong sewing enthusiast and crafter, she has written and edited numerous books, including several titles in the *Singer Sewing Reference Library*, *Sewing 101*, *Quilting 101*, and *Home Décor Sewing 101*.

CAROL PILOT has made a career out of being creative. She designs sewing and craft projects as well as interior décor items and displays for special events.

JOANNE WAWRA is the project and photo stylist for Creative Publishing. With a background in textiles and fashion merchandising, Joanne selects the fabrics and notions for the projects in the Lifestyles books and works alongside the photographer to create the beautiful photos.

CAROL ZENTGRAF is a designer and writer for the craft and sewing industries and a member of the Society of Creative Designers. She is the author of two home décor sewing books and numerous articles for several leading sewing and embroidery magazines.

Sources

Beacon Adhesives Company, Inc.
(800) 865-7238
www.beaconcreates.com
Quilter's Choice basting glue

Colorful Quilts and Textiles
2233 Energy Park Drive, Suite 400
Saint Paul, MN 55108
(651) 628-9664
www.colorfulquiltsandtextiles.com
hand-dyed tops by Diane Bartels

Delta Technical Coatings
(800) 423-4135
www.deltacrafts.com
acrylic paints and mediums
www.deltacrafts.com/
rubberstampede
*provided the chunky foam stamp
Polk-A-Dot Tulip #CHS 19064 on
page 33 and the Acanthus
Background stamp #3320R on
page 59*

Dharma Trading Company
P.O. Box 150916
San Raphael, CA 94915
(800) 542-5227
email: catalog@dharmatrading.com
www.dharmatrading.com
*dyes, paints, fabrics, and supplies for
coloring fabric*

Fire Mountain Gems and Beads
One Fire Mountain Way
Grants Pass, OR 97526-2373
(800) 423-2319
www.firemountaingems.com
beads and beading materials

Hot Potatoes
www.hotpotatoes.com
*provided the Grape Leaf stamp
#L113 on page 122*

Moondance Color Company
622 Spencer Road
Oakham, MA 01068
(508) 882-3383
www.moondancecolor.com
*felted wool, rug hooking fabrics,
and supplies*

Roc-lon Industries
www.roc-lon.com
*information about blackout drapery
lining*

Rupert, Gibbon & Spider, Inc.
P. O. Box 425
Healdsburg, CA 95448
(800) 442-0455
www.jacquardproducts.com
dyes, paints, and fabric

Silkpaint Corporation
18220 Waldron Drive
P.O. Box 18 INT
Waldron, MO 64092
(800) 563-0074
www.silkpaint.com
rayon/silk velvet

Sunbelt Fastener Co.
8841 Exposition Boulevard
Culver City, CA
email: info@sunbeltfastener.com
(800) 642-6587
www.sunbeltfastener.com
purse hardware and handles

Tandy Leather Company
P.O. Box 791
Fort Worth, TX 76101
800-433-3201 Ext. 1317
www.tandyleather.com
leather and suede

Thai Silks
252 State Street
Los Altos, CA 94022
(800) 221-7455 (California)
(800) 722-7455 (Elsewhere in
the U.S.)
www.thaisilks.com
silk fabrics

Therm O Web
770 Glenn Avenue
Wheeling, IL 60090
(874) 520-5200
www.thermoweb.com/consumer.html
iron-on vinyl